Ginn
Mathematics 3

TEXTBOOK 2

Parallel and perpendicular.

1

AB and CD are parallel.
EF is perpendicular to AB and to CD.
(a) Measure EF.
(b) Measure some other perpendicular distances between the lines.
What do you notice?

2 (a) Draw two parallel lines.
Measure the perpendicular distance between them in several places.
What do you notice?
(b) Repeat with other pairs of parallel lines.

3

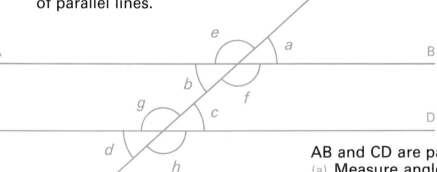

AB and CD are parallel.
(a) Measure angles *a*, *b*, *c* and *d*.
What do you notice?
(b) Measure angles *e*, *f*, *g* and *h*.
What do you notice?

4 (a) Draw a pair of parallel lines with a line across them.
See if your results from question 3 are the same for your new angles.
(b) Repeat with other sets of lines.

Line of symmetry.

Some shapes have more than one line of symmetry.
Here is how to complete a shape with four lines of symmetry.

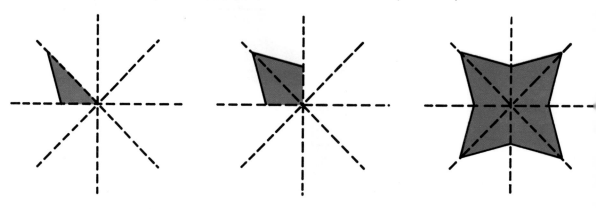

The dashed lines are lines of symmetry.
Trace the shapes and draw the parts that are missing.

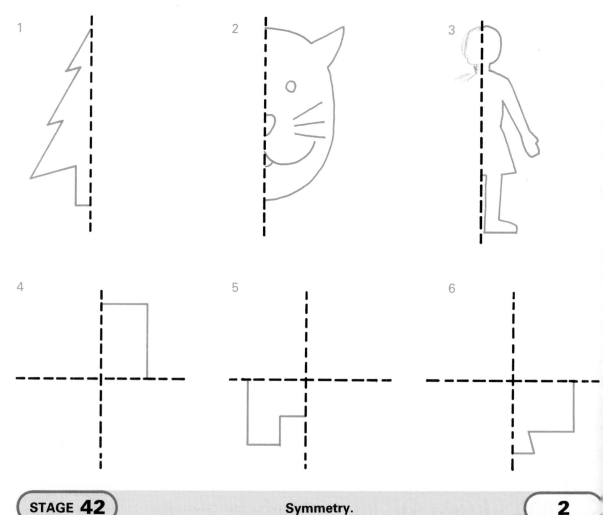

1

2

3

4

5

6

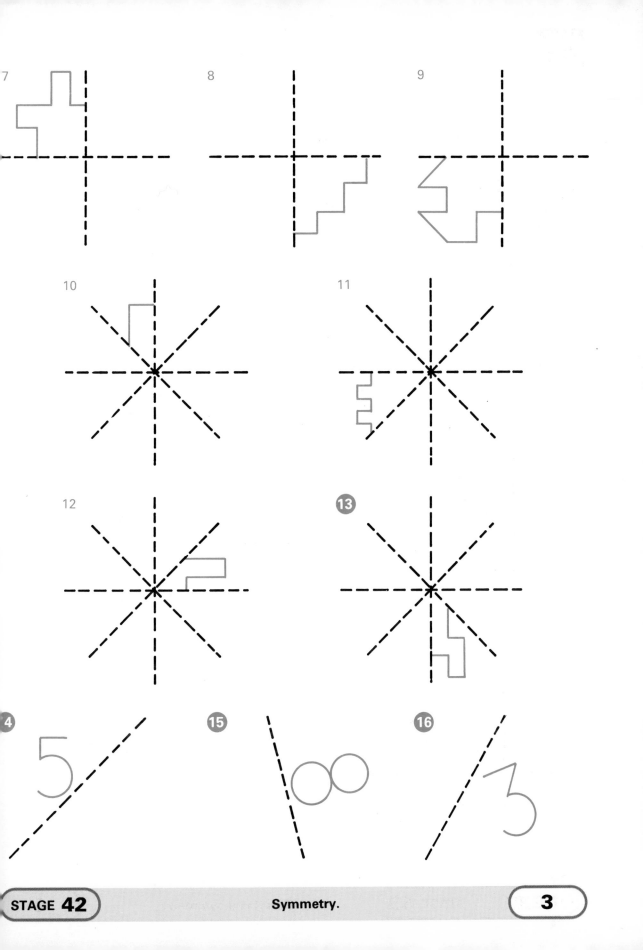

Susan has made a tracing of the square.
She found four ways of fitting the tracing onto the square without turning over the tracing paper.
We say the square has **rotational symmetry of order 4**.

1   Give the order of symmetry for these shapes.

(a) 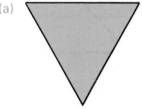   (b) 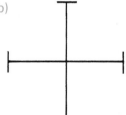   (c)

(d)    (e)    (f)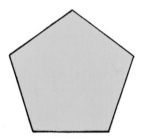

(g)    (h)    (i)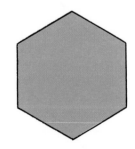

2   **Draw different shapes that have rotational symmetry of these orders.**

(a) **2**   (b) **3**   (c) **4**   (d) **5**

A B C D E F G H I J K L M
N O P Q R S T U V W X Y Z

Altaf traced this alphabet on tracing paper.

He turned the tracing paper to find the order of rotational symmetry for each letter.

The letters A, B, C and D only fitted once.

This means that they have **rotational symmetry of order 1**.

Some letters fitted twice. They have **rotational symmetry of order 2**.

1 Which of the letters above have:

   (a)   rotational symmetry of order 2?

   (b)   rotational symmetry of order 1?

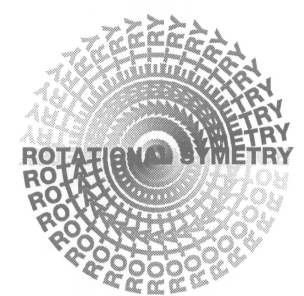

2 Which of the digits below have

   (a)   rotational symmetry of order 2?

   (b)   rotational symmetry of order 1?

0 1 2 3 4 5 6 7 8 9

keeping skills sharp

1	$48 + 79$	2	$136 + 64$	3	$285 + 686$	4	$592 + 177$
5	$70 - 23$	6	$111 - 48$	7	$602 - 313$	8	$500 - 142$

Triangles and quadrilaterals.

Here are some triangles (three-sided shapes)
and quadrilaterals (four-sided shapes).

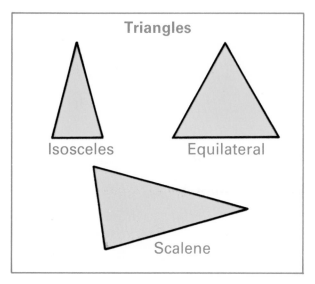

Triangles

Isosceles   Equilateral

Scalene

1 Which triangle has:

(a) no two sides equal?

(b) all three sides equal?

(c) only two sides equal?

(d) all three angles equal?

(e) two equal angles?

(f) no lines of symmetry?

(g) one line of symmetry?

(h) three lines of symmetry?

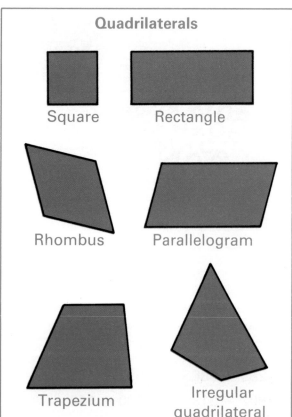

Quadrilaterals

Square   Rectangle

Rhombus   Parallelogram

Trapezium   Irregular
quadrilateral

2 Study the clues. Then name the
quadrilateral.

(a) 4 sides are equal.
All 4 angles are not equal.

(b) 4 equal sides.
4 equal angles.

(c) 2 pairs of equal sides.
4 equal angles.

(d) Only 1 pair of parallel sides.

③ How many of the quadrilaterals
shown have lines of symmetry?
(*Warning!* The answer is **not** 4.)

④ Can you draw a quadrilateral that
has just one line of symmetry?

Drawing rectangles and squares.

You can draw right angles with a protractor or a set square.

1 Follow these steps and draw a rectangle with sides 8 cm and 3 cm.

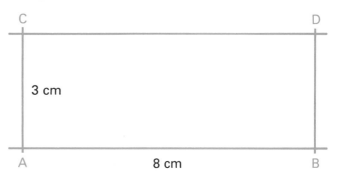

Step 1. Draw a line and mark two points 8 cm apart. Call these A and B.

Step 2. Use a set square or a protractor and draw right angles at A and B.

Step 3. On the lines at right angles to AB mark lengths of 3 cm. Call the points C and D.

Step 4. Join C and D to complete the rectangle ABCD.

2 Draw rectangles with sides of these lengths.
   (a) 10 cm and 6 cm   (b) 4 cm and 9 cm
   (c) 8.5 cm and 7 cm   (d) 50 mm and 65 mm

3 Draw squares with sides of these lengths.
   (a) 7 cm   (b) 10 cm   (c) 8.5 cm

4 Calculate the perimeters of the rectangles in question 2.

5 Calculate the perimeters of the squares in question 3.

6 A rectangular lawn measures 10 metres by 7.5 metres.
   (a) Draw a plan of the lawn with 1 cm representing 1 m.
   (b) Calculate the perimeter of (i) the plan, (ii) the lawn.

Drawing triangles.

Draw a triangle ABC with the sides 6 cm, 7 cm and 8 cm long.

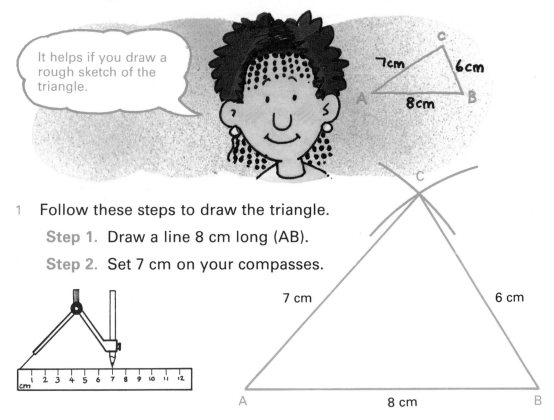

It helps if you draw a rough sketch of the triangle.

1   Follow these steps to draw the triangle.

   Step 1. Draw a line 8 cm long (AB).

   Step 2. Set 7 cm on your compasses.

   Step 3. Put your compass point on A and make an arc.

   Step 4. Set the compasses at 6 cm.

   Step 5. Put the compass point on B and make an arc to cut the arc you drew in **Step 3**. Where the arcs meet is point C.

   Step 6. Join C to A and to B.

   ABC is the triangle.

2   Draw these triangles.
    Draw a rough sketch first.
    (a) 9 cm, 5 cm, 5 cm   (b) 7 cm, 6 cm, 3 cm
    (c) 8.5 cm, 4 cm, 6 cm   (d) 75 mm, 75 mm, 50 mm

3   Calculate the perimeters of the triangles in question 2.

4   Can you draw a triangle with sides 9 cm, 3 cm and 4 cm?
    If not, why not?

Polyominoes.

A

B

Shapes made by joining squares to fit along their edges are called **polyominoes**. (Dominoes have two squares. 'Poly' means 'many'. These words have been put together to make a new word.)

If you cut out shape A, you could lift it up and turn it over to fit on shape B. But you cannot keep shape A flat and turn it round to fit on shape B.

On this page, count shapes like these as the same:
- shapes that can be kept flat and turned round to fit on another shape;
- shapes that can be lifted up and turned over to fit on another shape.

P

Q

R

S

1   Which shape is the same as (a) P?   (b) Q?

   (c)   How many different polyominoes can be made by joining three squares?

2   Five polyominoes can be made with four squares. Draw the other two.

3   You need some cubes.

   Find how many different shapes you can make by joining three cubes so they are joined at a face.

4   Work with some friends. See how many shapes you can make with four cubes.

Prisms and pyramids.

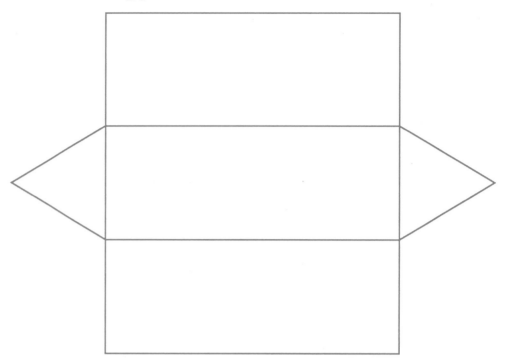

1 Trace the shape above. It is the net of a **triangular prism**.

Cut out your tracing and fold it to make the prism. Use sticky tape to keep the faces in position. The prism will look like this.

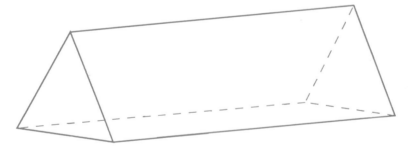

Lines like this _ _ _ _ _ _ _ _ show edges that are out of sight.

2 This is a **rectangular prism**. It is also called a cuboid.

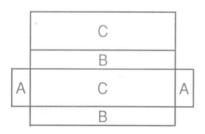

Check that

A measures $\frac{1}{2}$ cm × 1 cm,

B measures $\frac{1}{2}$ cm × 4 cm,

C measures 1 cm × 4 cm.

Draw a net like the one above, but with sides 4 times as long (2 cm, 4 cm, 16 cm). Cut it out and make the cuboid.

This is the net of a
square-based pyramid.

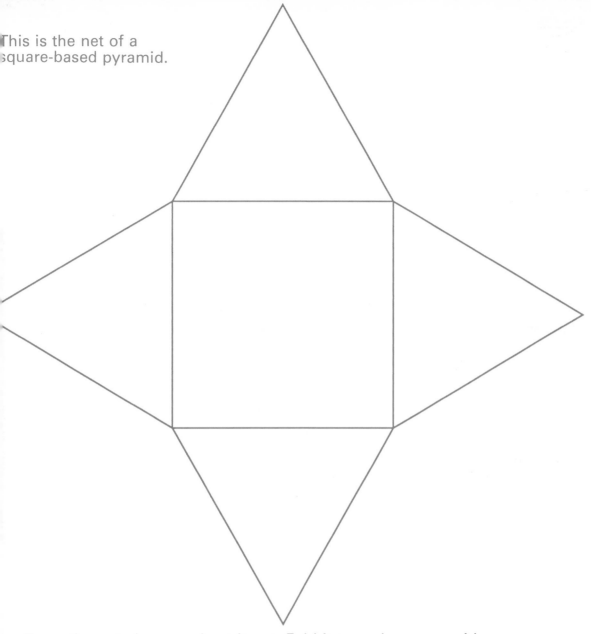

3   Trace the net above and cut it out. Fold it to make a pyramid.

(a)   What do you notice about the lengths of the eight edges of your
     pyramid?

(b)   The square forms the base. What is the shape of the other four faces?

4   Your teacher will show you how to draw an equilateral triangle using
   compasses, pencil and ruler.

   This is the net of a pyramid with a
   triangular base. Copy this net, but make
   the edges 7 cm. Fold the net to make the
   pyramid.

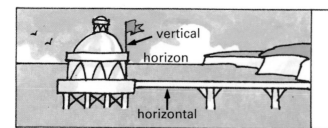

A **horizontal** line is one that is parallel to the horizon.
A **vertical** line is one that is at right angles to the horizon.

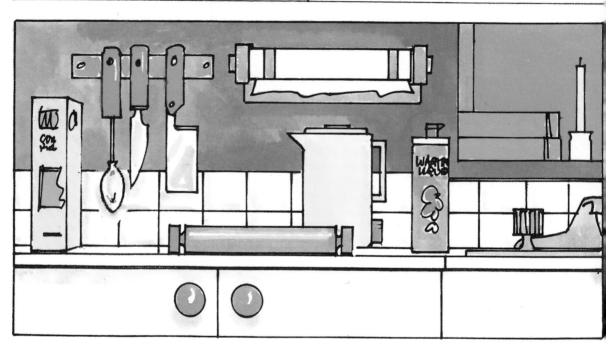

1   Imagine you are in the kitchen shown above.
    List things that are: (a) horizontal;   (b) vertical.

2   (a) List things in your classroom that are horizontal.
    (b) List things in your classroom that are vertical.

3   A carpenter uses a spirit-level to see if a shelf is horizontal.
    Make your own spirit-level by filling a bottle
    nearly full of water, but leaving a small space
    to make an air bubble.
    Find out how to use it, then check things in
    your classroom to see if they are horizontal.

4   A plumb-line can be used to see if the edge of a bookcase is vertical.
    Make a plumb-line by hanging a heavy object, such as a key,
    from the end of a piece of thread.
    Use it to check things in your classroom that seem to be vertical.

0        $\frac{1}{2}$ 1

No chance   Poor chance   Even chance   Good chance   Certain

There is **no chance** that you will grow an extra head.

It is **certain** that New Year's Day will follow New Year's Eve.

Answer these using one of the five choices at the top of this page.

1   I will go to sleep tonight.

2   It will rain tomorrow.

3   If I toss a coin, it will land 'heads'.

4   I will eat an orange within the next 24 hours.

5   I will run my own shop before I am 50 years old.

6   I will have a bath on Saturday or Sunday.

7   My teacher next year will be more than 70 years old.

8   $14 \times 8 = 102$

9   All women were once girls.

10   All boys will become men.

11   If I roll two dice, the total they show will be 3 or less.

Experimental probability.

Two pupils put some red, yellow and blue marbles in the bag.
One pupil mixed up the marbles and the other, without looking in the bag, took out a marble and recorded its colour.
The marble was replaced in the bag and the experiment repeated.
Here is the record they kept of the experiment.

Experiment: picking a marble from a bag.			
Possible colours	⚪	⚫	🔴
Tally of colours picked	ⅢⅢ Ⅲ	ⅢⅠ	ⅢⅢ ⅢⅢ Ⅱ
Fraction for each colour	$\frac{8}{24}$	$\frac{4}{24}$	$\frac{12}{24}$

1 How many times was a marble picked out of the bag?

2 How many times was a yellow marble picked?

3 How many times was a blue marble picked?

4 What fraction of the marbles picked were red?

5 If you had to guess, would you guess that there were more blue marbles in the bag, or more yellow marbles?

6 Use some red, yellow and blue marbles.
   Repeat the experiment described above,
   then answer questions 1 to 5 from your results.

7 Do your results differ from those of the two pupils?
   If so, can you suggest why?

Experiment: tossing a drawing pin.		
Possible results		
Tally	‖‖ ‖‖ ‖‖ ‖‖	‖‖ ‖‖
Fraction of all the tosses	$\overline{25}$	$\overline{25}$

8 How many tosses were made?

9 How many times did the drawing pin land (a) 'point down'? (b) 'point up'?

10 What fraction of the drawing pins landed 'point up'?

11 If you were to toss the drawing pin once, which is the most likely result — 'point down' or 'point up'?

12 Toss a penny 40 times and complete this record of your experiment.

Possible results		
Tally		
Fraction of all tosses		

Andrew tossed a paper cup and recorded the results on a bar graph.

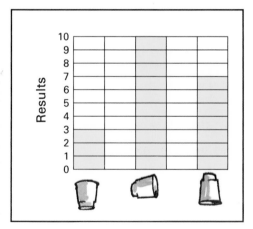

13 How many different positions did the cup land in?

14 How many times did he toss the cup?

15 What fraction of the results were 'right way up'?

16 If you were to toss the cup once, how would it be most likely to land?

Measure the length of these lines (a) in millimetres, (b) in centimetres.

1

2

3

Bar charts, bar-line graphs and line graphs.

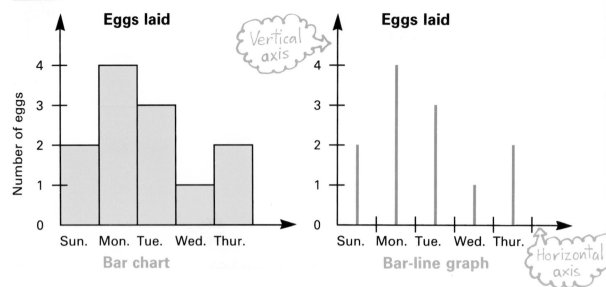

When each bar of a **bar chart** is made very narrow, it become a line. We then have a **bar-line graph**.

Note that the lines are drawn through the mid-points of the bars.

1   The table below gives the number of pupils absent each day from a class of 30.

Day	Mon.	Tue.	Wed.	Thur.	Fri.
Number absent	6	2	3	4	5

Use 2 cm to represent each day on the horizontal axis.

Use 2 cm to represent each pupil absent on the vertical axis.

(a)   What length will represent the pupils absent on

(i) Monday?   (ii) Tuesday?   (iii) Wednesday?

(iv) Thursday?   (v) Friday?

(b)   Draw a bar-line graph to show the pupils absent.

(c)   What is the total number of pupils absent in the week?

(d)   How many more were absent on Friday than on Wednesday?

(e)   How many pupils were present each day?

2   Keep a record of how many pupils are absent each day from your class for a week. Answer question 1 again for your class.

Line graph showing temperatures.

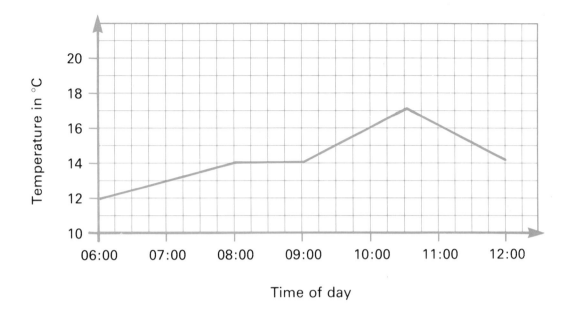

Time of day

The temperatures at each hour have been joined by straight lines to give a **line graph**.

Answer the following questions from the graph.

1 What was the temperature at
  (a) 06:00?   (b) 09:00?   (c) 10:00?   (d) 12:00?

2 What was
  (a) the maximum temperature?
  (b) the minimum temperature?

3 What happened to the temperature between 08:00 and 09:00?

4 (a) What is the time mid-way between 10:00 and 11:00?
  (b) What was the temperature at that time?

5 At what time was the temperature
  (a) 15 °C?   (b) 13.5 °C?   (c) 12.5 °C?

6 Collect temperatures each hour from 09:00 to 16:00. Use the same scales as for the line graph at the top of this page and plot your own line graph.

  Make up questions like those above and answer them from your graph.

Reading a thermometer.

There are many different kinds of thermometers. Unless you use the right kind, you could break it.

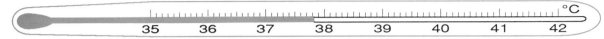

This is a clinical thermometer. It is used to measure a patient's temperature. The mercury shows what the temperature is.

The thermometer above shows 37.8 °C.

A healthy person has a temperature of about 37 °C.

A temperature of 40.5 °C would tell a doctor the patient was not well and together with other symptoms give guidance as to what the illness was.

Other thermometers may only indicate each degree mark.

You can estimate the temperature to one place of decimals.

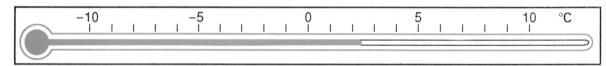

The reading on this thermometer is approximately 2.3 °C.

Give the following readings to one decimal place.

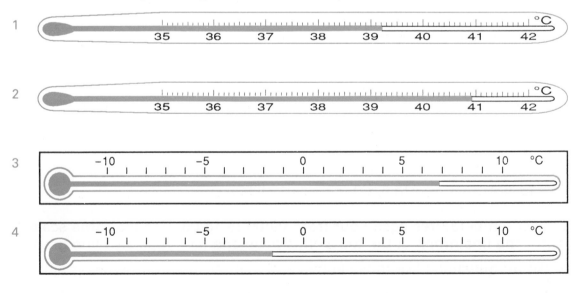

5　In question 1 what would the temperature be if it

(a)　rose 3.8 °C?　　　　(b)　dropped 1.5 °C?

6　In question 3 what would the temperature be if it

(a)　rose 3 °C?　　　　(b)　rose 2.7 °C?

(c)　fell 0.9 °C?　　　　(d)　fell 2.4 °C?

7

Hot water　　　Warm water　　　Cold water

You could do this experiment at home.
Put one hand into hot water and the other into cold water.
Leave them there for about a minute.
Put both hands into a bowl of warm water.
What do you notice?

8　Ask your teacher to pour some very hot water into a bowl.
Use a suitable thermometer and take the temperature of the water.
Record it.
Take the temperature of the water every 5 minutes for the next 40 minutes.
Record each temperature.

Discuss a suitable scale with your teacher and draw a line graph to show your results.

From your graph estimate the temperature after

(a)　$2\frac{1}{2}$ minutes;　　　(b)　$17\frac{1}{2}$ minutes;　　　(c)　$32\frac{1}{2}$ minutes.

A line graph of a patient's temperature.

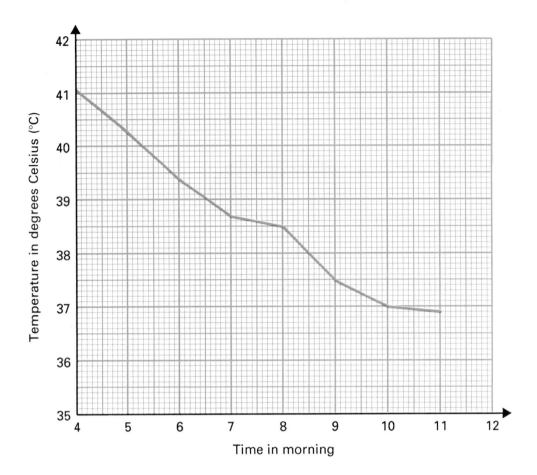

The graph shows the temperature of a patient, taken every hour.

1   What was the patient's temperature at

   (a)   5 a.m.?   (b)   7 a.m.?   (c)   11 a.m.?

The graph shows an **estimated** temperature in between the hours.

2   What is the estimated temperature at

   (a)   5:30 a.m.?   (b)   7:30 a.m.?   (c)   8:30 a.m.?

3   What is the fall in temperature between

   (a)   4:00 a.m. and 7:00 a.m.?   (b)   6:00 a.m. and 11:00 a.m.?

4   Find the approximate time when the patient's temperature is estimated as

   (a)   40 °C;   (b)   38 °C;   (c)   39.2 °C;   (d)   37.8 °C.

Do you watch more television
than your classmates?

Conduct a survey to find out how
many minutes of television each
of your classmates watched
yesterday. Round each person's
time to the nearest 30 minutes.

Show your results on a bar graph.
Use a grid like the one shown.

(a) How many pupils watched
more than you did?
(b) How many watched less than
you did?

What was the average number of
minutes spent watching
television?

(a) How many pupils watched
more than the average?
(b) How many watched less than
the average?

Find out which day your
classmates watch most television.
Draw a bar graph for that day.
Give some reasons why they
watch most television that day.
If the graph you drew in question 2
was for the most popular day, draw
one for the next most popular day.

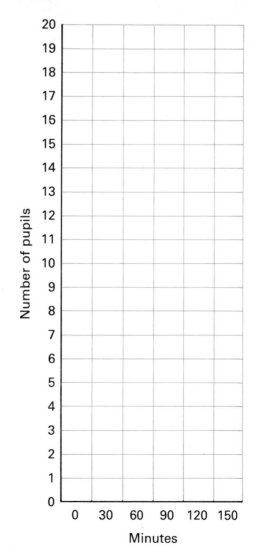

Number of pupils

Minutes

Collecting and recording information.

1 (a) List the months of the year.
       Ask each pupil in the class which month they were born in.
       Make a record of this by using tallies.
       Find the total for each month.
       Your result may look like this:

       July   ⅢⅡ I   6

   (b) Choose a suitable scale for a bar-line graph to show the birthday
       months. Discuss it with your teacher, then draw the graph.

   (c) In which month were most pupils born?

   (d) In which months were no pupils born?

   (e) Find the difference between the number born in October and in March.

2 (a) Use tallies and collect from your classmates the number of children in
       their family.

       Find the total of the tallies for each number of children.
       The numbers will be 1, 2, ... up to the largest number in a family.
       Draw a bar-line graph to represent the number.
       Put the possible number of children (1, 2, . . .) on the horizontal axis.
       Put the number of tallies for each on the vertical axis.

   (b) What is the total number of children?

   (c) What is the average number of children in a family?
       (You can use a calculator to work this out.)

Work with some friends. Your teacher will tell you which of the projects you can do in school time.

Others you may do after school, or at the weekend.

For each project you need to:

(a)   Collect the data, using tallies.

(b)   Add the tallies. The total is called the **frequency**.

(c)   Draw a graph to represent the information collected.

(d)   Make up questions based on the information. Exchange these with other pupils. They answer your questions, you answer theirs.

Some topics to choose from:

- Number of days a week when shoppers to to a particular shop.

- Favourite make of trainer.

- Favourite pop-record in the current top twenty. (Can you predict which records are moving towards the No. 1 spot?)

- Most popular sweet or chocolate bar.

- Eye colours – brown, hazel, grey, green, blue.

- Amount of time spent travelling to school.

- Most hated TV commercial.

- Favourite type of crisps.

Think of some other topics to collect information about.

Frequency graphs.

This is a tally chart showing the number
of cars in a school car park.

	Tally of cars	Frequency
9 a.m.	IIII IIII III	13
10 a.m.	IIII IIII IIII	15
11 a.m.	IIII IIII II	12
12 noon	IIII IIII	10
1 p.m.	IIII I	6

The total number of tallies
for any one time is called
the **frequency**.

A graph with the frequencies on the vertical axis is called
a **frequency** graph.

1 Plot a frequency graph for the information at the top of this page.
   Use 2 cm to represent each hour on the horizontal axis.
   Use 1 cm to represent each car on the vertical axis.
   Join each point by a straight line to give a line graph.

2 Use your graph to answer these questions:

   (a) When are there most cars in the car park?

   (b) What happens to the number of cars at 1:00 p.m.?

3 Use your common sense to answer these questions:

   (a) Why does the graph line suddenly drop between 12:00 noon and
        1:00 p.m.?

   (b) Why is there a peak at 10:00 a.m.?

4 Collect information from your classmates and draw a frequency graph to
   show the number of pets their families have. Make up questions based on
   the graph and give them to friends to answer. You answer your friends'
   questions.

A **number pair** is used to locate a point on a grid.

To locate point A we start at 0 and count 5 units to the right. Then we count 3 units up.

To give the location of point A, we use the number pair (5,3). The first number tells us the number of units to the right and the second number tells us the number of units up.

Number pairs are called **coordinates**. The coordinates of A are (5,3).

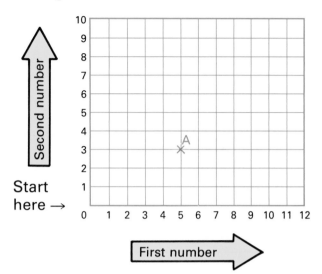

1 Make a grid like the one shown. Plot these points on your grid.

A	(7,4)	B	(12,4)
C	(10,1)	D	(4,1)
E	(2,4)	F	(6,4)
G	(6,5)	H	(2,5)
I	(6,12)	J	(12,5)
K	(6,5)	L	(6,14)
M	(8,14)	N	(7,13)
O	(8,12)	P	(6,12)

Join the points in alphabetical order. What do you get a picture of?

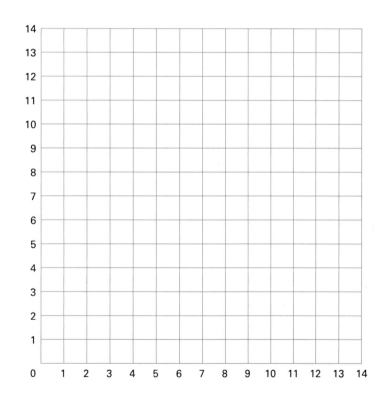

2 Make another grid like the one in question 1.
  (a) Put these points on your grid:
      (12,8) (12,12) (8,12) (8,8)
      Join the points in the same order
      and the last point to the first point.
      What shape have you made?
  Do the same for each of these:
  (b) (0,8) (4,8) (2,4)
  (c) (1,11) (1,14) (7,14) (7,11)
  (d) (6,6) (12,6) (8,2) (2,2)
  (e) (12,0) (14,2) (12,4) (10,2)

3 Plot the points of these coordinates.
  (0,3) (1,4) (2,5) (3,6)
  (4,7) (5,8) (6,9)
  Join them.
  What do you notice?

4

First number	1	2	3	4	5	6	7	8	9	10
Second number	0	1	2	3						

  (a) When the first number is 1, the second number is 0. If you change the firs[t]
      number to 2, the second number will change to 1, and so on.
      Can you see the rule for the second number?
  (b) Copy and complete the table.
  (c) Plot the points and join them.
  (d) What do you notice?

5 On a new grid, draw a picture using straight lines.
  Work out the coordinates for your picture.
  Swap your list of coordinates with a friend.
  Draw each other's pictures.

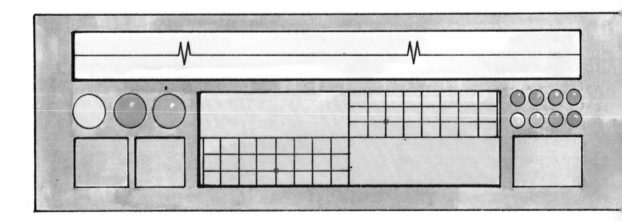

Coordinate game.

This game is for two players.
You need two dice, preferably in two colours.
Suppose these are blue and red (mark them with blue
and red ink if you have only got white dice).

Draw two grids on squared paper, one for each player.

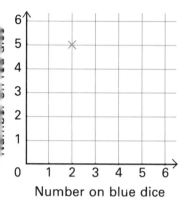

Number on blue dice

Each player rolls one of the dice.
The player with the higher
number starts the game.

The number on the blue dice shows
the number of units to the right.
The number on the red dice shows the
number of units up.

The point marked is (2,5) so the
number on the blue dice was 2 and the number
on the red dice was 5.
The players take it in turns to throw the dice.
They plot their own points on their grids.
The first player to get three points in a
straight line is the winner.
The points can be in a horizontal,
vertical or diagonal line.
They need not be next to each other.
Here are some examples of winning lines.

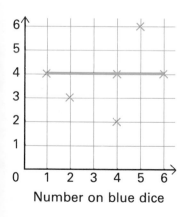

Number on blue dice

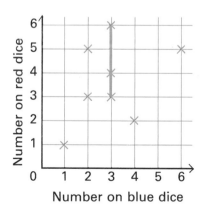

Number on blue dice

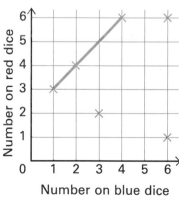

Number on blue dice

Using BASIC.

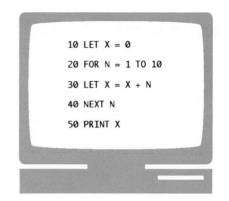

```
10 LET X = 0
20 FOR N = 1 TO 10
30 LET X = X + N
40 NEXT N
50 PRINT X
```

This program will add together 10 consecutive numbers.

`10 LET X = X + N`

This line gives X a new value which is equal to its old value plus the present value of N.

When this program is run each time the value of N is increased it is added on to the previous total.

Complete this table with values of N from 1 to 10:

Old value of X	Value of N	New value of X (old X + N)
0	1	1
1	2	3
3	3	6
6	4	

1 By changing line 20, add together the first 15 numbers.

2 In the song 'The Twelve Days of Christmas' how many gifts were given on the twelfth day?

3 By changing lines 10 and 20 add together all the numbers from 11 to 18.

Triangular numbers

By making a slight alteration to the program could you print out the first 10 triangular numbers?

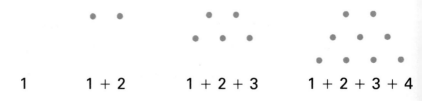

1   1 + 2   1 + 2 + 3   1 + 2 + 3 + 4

Random numbers in BASIC.

In our BASIC programs so far we have given numbers to the program by
either   `LET X = 3`
  or   `INPUT X`   (when you type in a value).

In BASIC we can make the computer choose a number. Try these two
programs to see which one works with your computer. The program will print
out ten dice throws.

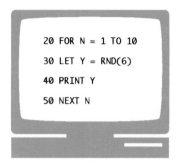

```
20 FOR N = 1 TO 10
30 LET Y = RND(6)
40 PRINT Y
50 NEXT N
```

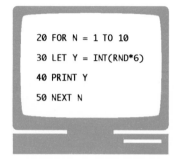

```
20 FOR N = 1 TO 10
30 LET Y = INT(RND*6)
40 PRINT Y
50 NEXT N
```

1   By changing line 30 let the random number chosen be between 1 and 25.

2   By adding line 35 could you make the number chosen be between 4 and 28?

Using random numbers allows you to write programs where different
numbers may appear each time.

```
10 LET A = RND(10)
20 LET B = RND(10)
30 PRINT A; "+"; B; "=";
40 INPUT Y
```

`30 PRINT A; "+"; B; "=";`

This line prints on the screen 7+3=
                                 or 8+5=
depending on the random numbers.

Everything inside " " is printed. This
could be words, numbers or symbols.

Line 40 waits until you type in an answer.

There are many changes you can now make to this program.

3   Make it produce multiplication bonds (change line 30).

4   Make it produce subtraction questions where the first number is between
    11 and 20, and the second from 1 to 10 (change 10 and 30).

5   Make it ask five questions each time it is run (add lines 5 and 45).

6   Make it **check** the answer that you type in (add line 50).

STAGE 56

More about graphs and averages.

How well a plant grows depends on such conditions
as the type of soil, the amount of water,
the temperature, and the amount of sunlight.

A class planted a sunflower seed in a large clay pot.
They kept the plant in the sunlight and
watered it every 3 days.
They kept this record of how the plant grew.

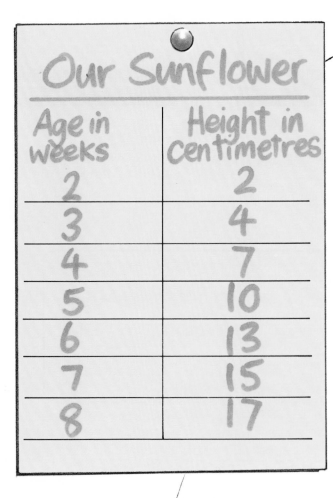

Our Sunflower

Age in weeks	Height in centimetres
2	2
3	4
4	7
5	10
6	13
7	15
8	17

1 Copy and complete the line graph of how the first sunflower grew.

The graph below shows the growth of a second sunflower that was given less water.

First sunflower

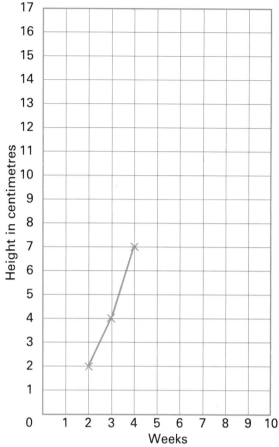

Second sunflower

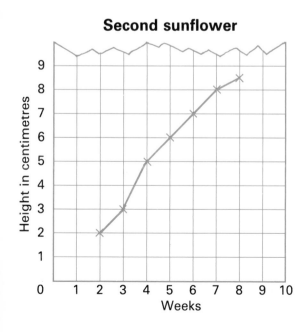

2 How tall was the second sunflower after 3 weeks?

3 How many weeks did it take for the second sunflower to become 7 cm tall?

4 How much did the second sunflower grow between the third and fourth weeks?

5 What was the difference in height between the two plants at the end of the fifth week?

6 Work with some classmates and grow some plants of your own. Keep a graph of your results.

Averages.

1 (a) Find out how many minutes each of your classmates spent reading after school yesterday.
Calculate the class average.

(b) Was the time you spent reading above or below the average?

2 (a) How many classmates read for less than the average time?

(b) How many read for more than the average time?

After-school playtime

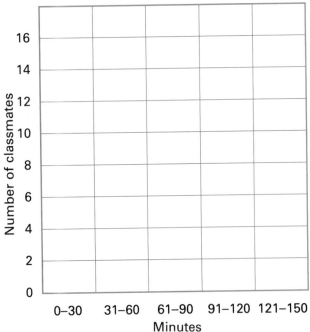

3 (a) Find the average amount of time your classmates spend playing after school.

(b) Copy the grid and make a graph of your findings.

1 You need a local map and a calculator.
Work with a friend and plan a walking trip.
You should plan to leave after breakfast and
arrive home well before it is dark. Choose
somewhere that interests you both, where
you can have a rest before returning home.
If it is too far to walk all the way you can go
part of the way by train or bus. From your
map find exactly how far you will be walking.
Find out the approximate cost of meals,
drinks and any fares. If you can, go on the
trip and keep a record of the actual distance
and costs. Note the times when you are
walking and when you are not. Use your
calculator to find your average speed by
dividing the total distance by the time you
were walking.

It is important
that you have permission
from your parents
or guardians.

2

Work with a friend.
Think of several things you like to eat.
Check the prices and the weights in as many
different shops as you can.
Work out which shop gives the best value.
You should use a calculator.
For example, the cost of 200 g of crystallized
pineapple is £1.60 in one shop and the cost
of 150 g is £1.10 in another shop.

The cost of 1 gram in the first shop is $\frac{160p}{200}$
or 0.8p and in the second shop

it is $\frac{110p}{150}$ or 0.7333333p.

So the second one is better value.

It is important
that you have permission
from your parents
or guardians.

3 Work with some friends.
You have to plan a car park for at least 50 cars.
You need to think carefully about the size of each rectangle
that a car parks in. (Measure some cars and allow for opening
the doors.) Also consider the width of the space between the
parking bays. If the road is not wide enough for two cars you
will need arrows to show a 'one-way' system.
Draw an accurate plan of your car park. Your teacher will help
you to decide the scale to use.
Draw up a suitable scale of parking charges to display at the
meters.

4 Think of something you would like to make out of paper or
card. For example it could be a model train, or a house, or a
castle, but you can please yourself.
Make a sketch of the pieces of paper or card that you would
need and put their measurements on them.

For example, this rectangle would make this cylinder

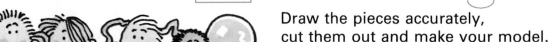

Draw the pieces accurately,
cut them out and make your model.

5 Plan a party for 10 people.
List what you will eat and drink
and how much it will cost.
Allow for any decorations and
prizes if you want to have them.

Decision trees.

A **decision tree** has decisions for you to make, generally by choosing 'Yes' or 'No'. It also branches out, as a tree does, which is why it is called a 'decision tree'.

This decision tree can be used to decide whether or not a shape is a square.

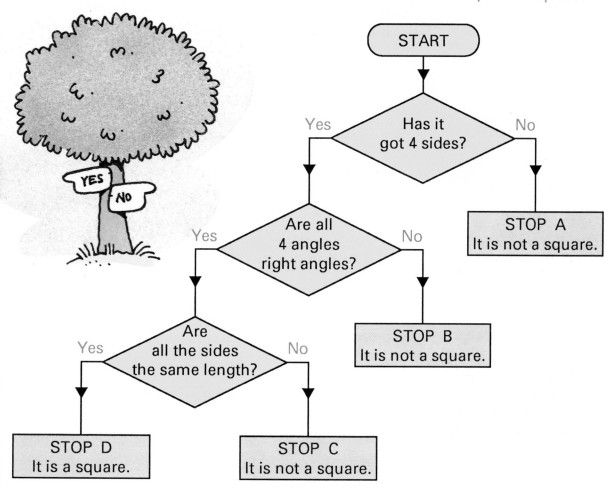

Use the decision tree above to decide which of these shapes are squares and which are not.

Give your answers as A, B, C or D according to which STOP the shape finishes at.

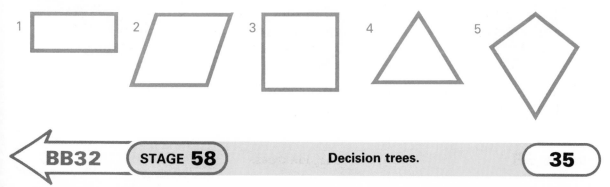

This is a decision tree to decide on what sort of animal you are thinking about.

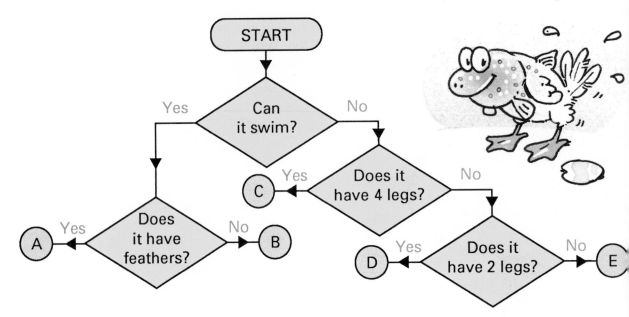

Use the decision tree above to answer these questions.
Give your answers as A, B, C, D or E in questions 1 and 2.

1   A duck would be in A. A fish would be in B.
    Where would you end up if you were thinking about

    (a) a tadpole?   (b) a swan?

2   Write the letter these would be in:

    (a) an octopus;   (b) a chicken;   (c) a table;   (d) you.

3   Name two animals, not given in question 2, that would be in:

    (a) B;   (b) C;   (c) D;   (d) E.

4   Make up your own decision tree for wild animals using the
    question boxes below.

Place these on your diagram: lion, crocodile, hippopotamus, monkey, fox,
rabbit.

Tossing coins.

What follows is a tree-diagram. (No decisions are made so it is not a decision tree.)

Get a coin. You are going to toss it.
Each time you toss the coin write
H for 'head' or T for 'tail'.

Head   Tail

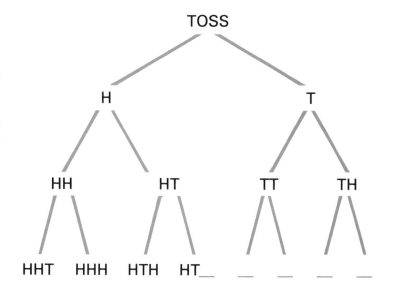

With one toss you might get a head or a tail.

With two tosses there are four possible results.

With three tosses there are eight possibilities.

1   Copy the diagram above and fill in the eight possibilities for three tosses.

2   Continue the tree diagram to show the sixteen possibilities when a coin is tossed four times.
    (Make sure you have a big sheet of paper!)

3   Use your answer to question 1 to copy and complete:

    The chance of getting two heads and one tail (in any order) from three tosses of a coin is __ out of 8.

4   Use your answer to question 2 to copy and complete:

    The chance of getting two heads and two tails from four tosses of a coin is __ out of ___.

Checking calculations.

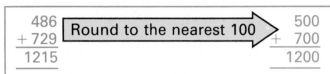

```
  486                                    500
+ 729   Round to the nearest 100      + 700
 1215                                   1200
```

The estimate (1200) is approximately equal to the exact answer (1215).

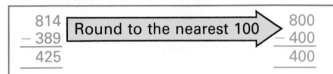

```
  814                                    800
- 389   Round to the nearest 100      - 400
  425                                    400
```

The estimate (400) is approximately equal to the exact answer (425).

Another way of checking subtraction is to add like this:

```
  814              389
- 389 ── add     + 425  ── This must equal the number you subtracted from.
  425              814  ←
```

You *could* check addition by subtracting, but there are better methods, such as rounding or adding 'up' instead of 'down'.

For example: 486 + 729 = 1215   1215 − 729 = 486   1215 − 486 = 729

1 Add these, then check your answers by adding 'up' each column.

(a)   139   (b)   583   (c)   146   (d)   208
    + 467   + 298   89   376
                                    + 367   + 95

2 Add these. Then check your answers by rounding each number to the nearest 100.

(a)   234   (b)   566   (c)   15   (d)   195
    + 498   324   477   496
                     + 688   + 384   + 204

3 Subtract these. Then check your answers by rounding.

(a)   304   (b)   211   (c)   524   (d)   800
    − 196   − 87   − 179   − 315

(e) 460 − 351   (f)   920 − 366   (g) 814 − 666

$91 \div 7 = 13$ You can check this by multiplying 7 and 13. $7 \times 13 = 91$

1   Divide these, then check your answers by multiplying.

   (a) $48 \div 6$ (b) $72 \div 8$ (c) $42 \div 2$ (d) $39 \div 3$

   (e) $85 \div 5$ (f) $84 \div 7$ (g) $48 \div 4$ (h) $81 \div 9$

2   Use a calculator to do these divisions, then to check by multiplying.

   (a) $126 \div 2$ (b) $294 \div 6$ (c) $702 \div 9$ (d) $460 \div 10$

   (e) $416 \div 8$ (f) $372 \div 4$ (g) $609 \div 7$ (h) $390 \div 5$

A possible calculator error

Use your calculator to divide 7 by 3. You will get 2.3333333.
Now multiply the 2.3333333 by 3. You will probably get 6.9999999 but
on some calculators you will get 7.
7 is the exact answer. Multiplying by 3, then dividing by 3 should
leave the original number unchanged.
If your calculator gives 6.9999999 you will have to round it up to 7.

---

3   Use your calculator to do these calculations.
    Round your answer to the nearest whole number if necessary.

   (a) $(7 \div 6) \times 12$ (b) $(13 \div 3) \times 9$ (c) $(29 \div 2) \times 4$

   (d) $(18 \div 7) \times 14$ (e) $(26 \div 6) \times 18$ (f) $(41 \div 11) \times 33$

4   Check your answers to question 3 by the simple calculations given below.
    Can you see how these simpler questions are obtained from those in
    question 3?
    Discuss your answer with your teacher.

   (a) 7×2 (b) 13×3 (c) 29×2

   (d) 18×2 (e) 26×3 (f) 41×3

Percentage.

Per cent (%) means the same as 'out of one hundred'.

70 of the small squares are blue; there are 100 small squares altogether.
70 per cent (70%) are blue.

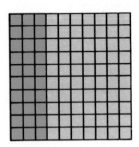

30 of the small squares are red.
As a fraction this is $\frac{30}{100}$ or $\frac{3}{10}$ (or 0.3).
As a percentage this is 30 per cent (30%).

There are 100 small squares in each of the larger squares.
Write the number of squares that are red:
(a) as a fraction with 100 as denominator;
(b) as a percentage.

1

2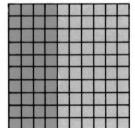

3

4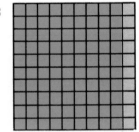

5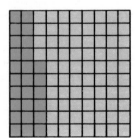

6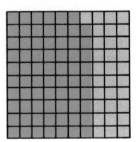

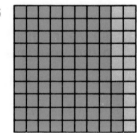

7   For each of the squares in questions 1 to 6 write down:
   (a) the fraction, with 100 as denominator, that is blue;
   (b) the percentage that is blue.

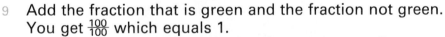

There are 100 small squares in this rectangle.
25 are green,
50 are yellow,
10 are purple.

8   Copy and complete this table.

	Fraction with denominator 100	Percentage
Green	$\frac{25}{100}$	25%
Not green	$\frac{75}{100}$	
Yellow		
Not yellow		
Purple		
Not purple		
Coloured	$\frac{85}{100}$	
Not coloured		

9   Add the fraction that is green and the fraction not green.
    You get $\frac{100}{100}$ which equals 1.
    (a) Add the fractions that are yellow and not yellow.
    (b) Add the fractions that are purple and not purple.
    (c) Add the fractions that are coloured and not coloured.
    (d) What do you notice about your answers to (a), (b) and (c)?

10 (a) Add the percentages that are green and not green.
    (b) Add the percentages that are yellow and not yellow.
    (c) Add the percentages that are purple and not purple.
    (d) Add the percentages that are coloured and not coloured.
    (e) What do you notice about your answers to (a), (b), (c) and (d)?

More about percentages.

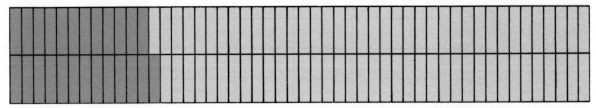

25 of the 100 rectangles are red.
As a percentage this is 25%.
As a fraction this is $\frac{25}{100}$ which equals $\frac{1}{4}$.
$25\% = \frac{25}{100} = \frac{1}{4}$.

1   Write these percentages as fractions in lowest terms.

(a)   **20%**   (b)   **50%**   (c)   **70%**   (d)   **2%**   (e)   **17%**

(f)   **16%**   (g)   **75%**   (h)   **80%**   (i)   **1%**   (j)   **5%**

2   Write these fractions with a denominator of 100 and as a percentage.

(a) $\frac{3}{10} = \frac{30}{100} = 30\%$ (b) $\frac{9}{10}$ (c) $\frac{1}{10}$ (d) $\frac{6}{10}$

(e) $\frac{7}{20}$ (f) $\frac{11}{20}$ (g) $\frac{9}{25}$ (h) $\frac{4}{25}$

(i) $\frac{17}{50}$ (j) $\frac{11}{50}$ (k) $\frac{1}{50}$ (l) $\frac{47}{50}$

To find 20% of 15 you divide 20 by 100 and then multiply by 15.

$20\% \text{ of } 15 = \frac{20}{100} \times 15 = 3$

$20\% \text{ of } 15 = \frac{1}{5} \times 15 = 3$

Ask your teacher for help if you don't understand how to do this.

$20\% = \frac{1}{5}$

3   Calculate.

(a)   **10% of 30**   (b)   **1% of 400**   (c)   **8% of 50**

(d)   **65% of 60**   (e)   **13% of 1000**   (f)   **35% of 120**

4   A sewing machine costs £140. A deposit of 15% has to be paid.
(a) How much is the deposit?
(b) How much still has to be paid after paying the deposit?

Discount.

10% discount means the marked price is reduced by 10%.

Discount = 10% of £380 = £$\frac{10}{100}$ × 380 = £38.

Amount paid = £380 − £38 = £342.

1   Calculate the discount and the amount paid.

(a)

15% discount

£120

(b)

5% discount

£30

(c)

10% discount

£35

(d)

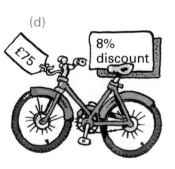

8% discount

£75

(e)

£25

12% discount

(f)

9% discount

£13

2   A car cost £5000. A discount of 12% was given.
(a) How much was the discount?   (b) How much was paid for the car?

3   A motorbike cost £1700. A discount of £170 was given.
(a) What percentage was the discount?
(b) How much was paid for the motorbike?

Calculate:

(a) the cost of these shopping bills before deducting discount.

(b) the amount of discount (rounded down).

(c) the cost of the bills after deducting discount.

1
2 tins of beans.
4 packets of cornflakes.
1 kg of sugar.

2
2 kg of sausages.
2 jars of jam.
3 loaves of bread.

3
2 kg of apples.
2 kg of sugar.
½ kg of sausages.

4
½ kg of apples.
3 tins of beans.
2 kg of sugar.

5
4 loaves of bread.
1½ kg of sausages.
3 packets of Corn Flakes

6
2 loaves of bread.
1 kg of sugar.
2 kg of sausages.
2 packets of Corn Flakes.

7
4 jars of jam.
¼ kg of sausages.
1½ kg of apples.
3 kg of sugar.

8
2½ kg of apples.
2 jars of jam.
1 packet of cornflakes.
½ kg of sausages.

Calculating prices.

Suppose that you want to find the
cost of 1 ball of wool.
Here is how to calculate the cost.

$$
\begin{array}{r}
29\frac{2}{3}\text{p each} \\
3\overline{)89\text{p}} \\
-60 \\
\hline
29 \\
-27 \\
\hline
2
\end{array}
$$

The exact price is $29\frac{2}{3}$p. Fractional prices are
rounded *up* to the next penny.
So the price of 1 ball of wool is 30p.

Find the price of one item.

1

2

3

4

Finding answers.

Jane and Robert travelled in Scotland with their parents.
Here are some questions about their trip.

1   Got up.

Left 1 hour 35 minutes later.
What time did they leave?

2   Stopped for petrol.
Tank holds 78 litres.

Took  to fill.

How much petrol was in the
tank before it was filled?

3   Looked at map.
How far did they have to go?

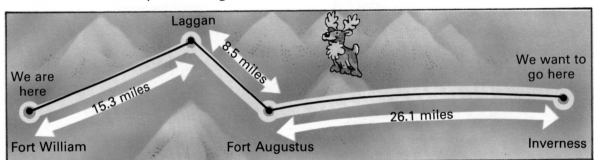

Laggan

8.5 miles

We want to
go here

We are
here

15.3 miles

26.1 miles

Fort William   Fort Augustus   Inverness

4   Stopped for snack.
   (a) Robert had:

£1.25

95p

49p

He gave the waitress
How much change?

(b) Jane had:

55p

38p

She gave the waitress
How much change?

5 Checked fuel gauge.
Tank holds 78 litres.
How much petrol is in the
tank?

6 Went fishing and
weighed the largest fish caught.
How much more did
Jane's fish weigh?

Jane's   Robert's

1.76 kg   0.98 kg

7 Saw road sign.
How far is it from Dingwall to
Invergordon?

Dingwall 25.9 miles

Invergordon 42.1 miles

8 Checked distance recorder.

Before trip 5 8 2 9 6 . 3

After trip   6 0 0 8 4 . 9

How many miles did they drive?

9 Went for a walk.

They walked 4.8 miles, then 19.7 miles. Then they stopped for a rest.
How much further must they go to walk a total of 30 miles?

Make up a story.

NUMBER NEWS

46.3 + 28.6 − 12.7 = 62.2

Who am I?

1. If you add 4 to me, the result is 11.

2. If you subtract 9 from me, the result is 5.

3. Multiply me by 6 and you get 48.

4. Multiply me by 10 and you get 120.

5. Divide me by 7 and you get 9.

6. Divide me by 6 and you get 12.

7. To get me, you multiply 5 by 13 and then subtract 10.

8. To get me, you divide 36 by 3 and then add 49.

9. If you double me and then subtract 5, you get 7.

10. If you halve me and then add 9, you get 17.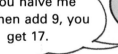

The multiply and add game.

Carol thinks of a number (1 to 10) to multiply by, then a number (1 to 10) to add.

Fred has to decide what Carol's numbers are.

Fred gives Carol a number, Carol gives Fred the result after multiplying and then adding with her two numbers.

Example

Carol has decided to multiply by 3 and add 5.

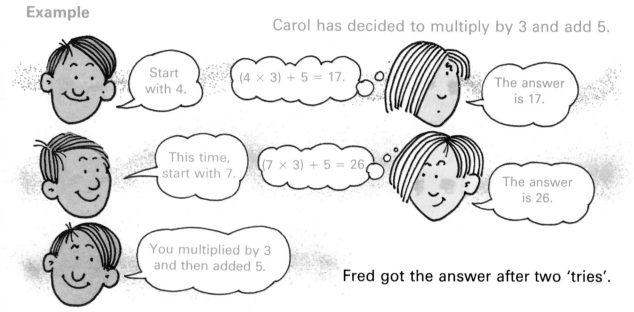

Start with 4.

$(4 \times 3) + 5 = 17.$

The answer is 17.

This time, start with 7.

$(7 \times 3) + 5 = 26.$

The answer is 26.

You multiplied by 3 and then added 5.

Fred got the answer after two 'tries'.

1   Play the game with a friend.
    Take it in turns to think of the numbers to multiply by and to add.
    See who takes the smaller number of tries to find the numbers.

2   **An investigation.**

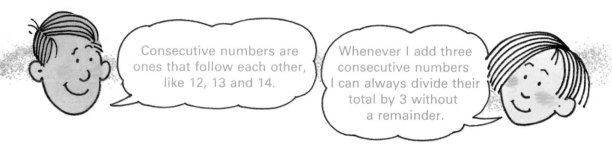

Consecutive numbers are ones that follow each other, like 12, 13 and 14.

Whenever I add three consecutive numbers I can always divide their total by 3 without a remainder.

You can use a calculator.
Add any three consecutive numbers and divide the total by 3. Was the division exact?
Do you think your answer is true for **any** three consecutive numbers?

Lengths and distances.

Remember these:

1 m = 100 cm	1 cm = 10 mm
1 m = 1000 mm	1 km = 1000 m

Copy and complete.

1   5 m = __ cm

2   150 cm = __ m

3   2500 m = __ km

4   11 cm = __ mm

5   1.4 m = __ mm

6   2.34 m = __ cm

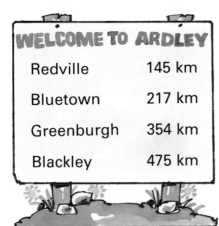

WELCOME TO ARDLEY

Redville	145 km
Bluetown	217 km
Greenburgh	354 km
Blackley	475 km

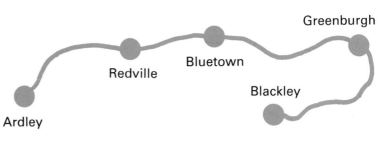

7   How far is it from Ardley to Blackley?

8   How far is it from Redville to Greenburgh?

9   How far is it from Greenburgh to Blackley?

Centimetre, metre or kilometre?
Which unit would you use to measure the following?

10   The length of a pencil.

11   The distance to the moon.

12   The height of a tall building.

13   The length of an aeroplane flight.

14   The length of a football pitch.

15   The thickness of a dictionary.

Copy and complete.

16   2 km = __ m

17   2.5 km = __ m

18   3.48 km = __ m

Project	Work in a group. Take it in turns to estimate in metres a distance in the school grounds. Keep a record of all the estimates. Then measure the distance to see who had the closest estimate. Try again with a different distance.

Length – addition and subtraction.

```
  4 m 27 cm        4.27 m
+3 m 85 cm       +3.85 m
  8 m 12 cm        8.12 m
```

```
   3
   ⁴m ¹⁰3 cm
 −1 m 12 cm
   2 m 91 cm
```

It's just like adding whole numbers, as long as you remember to regroup.

1 m is 100 cm

```
   3  1
   ⁴.03 m
 −1.12 m
   2.91 m
```

Add.

1. 3.67 cm
   +1.43 cm

2. 7.92 cm
   +4.83 cm

3. 2.41 km
   + 1.87 km

4. 3.05 km
   + 3.98 km

5. 5 m 24 cm
   +3 m 80 cm

6. 7 m 60 cm
   +9 m 78 cm

7. 3 cm 8 mm
   +4 cm 9 mm

8. 2 m 90 cm
   + 6 m 75 cm

Subtract.

9. 4.81 cm
   −1.92 cm

10. 5.04 km
    −3.76 km

11. 8.13 km
    − 7.39 km

12. 2.05 km
    − 0.40 km

13. 5 cm 6 mm
    −2 cm 9 mm

14. 8 m 42 cm
    − 6 m 60 cm

15. 4 m 67 cm
    −2 m 81 cm

16. 9 m 48 cm
    − 4 m 60 cm

17 Add 17.38 m, 12.74 m and 3.12 m.

18 Find the difference between: (a) 2.24 km and 0.80 km;
    (b) 9 cm 2 mm and 2 cm 6 mm.

Perimeters (revision).

The distance around a shape is called the **perimeter** of the shape.

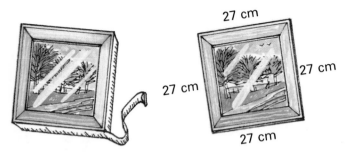

The perimeter of the picture is 108 cm.

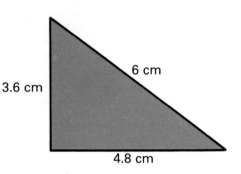

The perimeter of a shape can be found by adding the lengths of its sides. The perimeter of this triangle is 14.4 cm (3.6 cm + 4.8 cm + 6 cm).

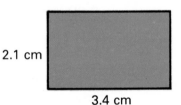

Perimeter of a rectangle = (length × 2) + (breadth × 2)
= (3.4 cm × 2) + (2.1 cm × 2)
= 6.8 cm + 4.2 cm
= 11.0 cm

Give the perimeter of each shape.

1
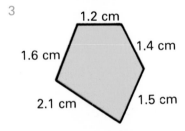

2
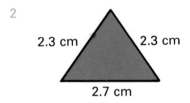

3
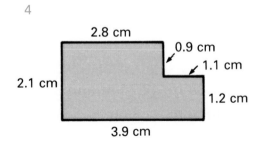

4

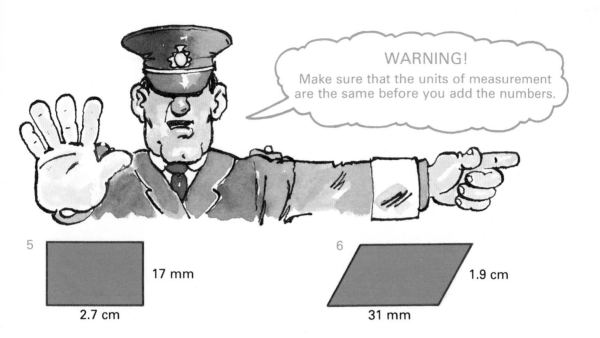

WARNING!
Make sure that the units of measurement are the same before you add the numbers.

5   17 mm
     2.7 cm

6   1.9 cm
     31 mm

Copy and complete these tables.

7

Squares	
Length of each side	Perimeter
32 mm	
15 mm	
2.5 cm	
5.25 m	

8

Rectangles		
Length	Breadth	Perimeter
4 cm	2 cm	
18 mm	1.2 cm	
12.4 m	7.6 m	
24.3 m	18.7 m	

9   Measure the length and breadth of a blackboard to the nearest centimetre. Calculate the perimeter.

10   Estimate the perimeter of your classroom to the nearest metre. Check your estimate by measuring.

11   The perimeter of a circle is called the **circumference** of the circle. Find a round object and measure its circumference.

12   How much fencing is needed for a rectangular field that is 185 m long and 76 m wide?

13   A square park has a perimeter of 6812 metres. How long is each side?

Volume.

To find the volume of a cuboid you first choose a unit.

1 cubic centimetre

How many
cubic centimetre
blocks will fill
this cuboid?

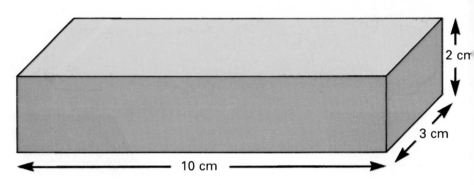

When you count the cubes you find that there are 60.

Is there a quicker
way to find the
volume of the
cuboid?

To find the volume
of a cuboid,
you can multiply:

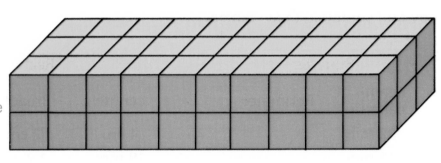

Volume = length × breadth × height

(*Remember*: breadth is the same as width.)

Volume = 10 cm × 3 cm × 2 cm.
Volume = 60 cubic centimetres.
Cubic centimetres can be written as cm³, so
Volume = 60 cm³

Volume = length × breadth × height
Volume = 5 cm × 3 cm × 1 cm
Volume = 15 cubic centimetres
          or 15 cm³

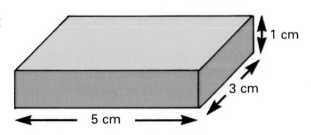

Give each volume. Be careful with the units – they will be cubic metres (m^3), cubic centimetres (cm^3), or cubic millimetres (mm^3).

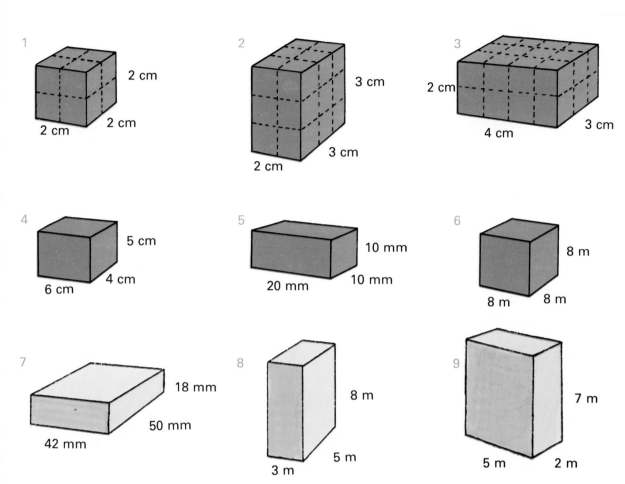

1 2 cm, 2 cm, 2 cm

2 3 cm, 3 cm, 2 cm

3 2 cm, 4 cm, 3 cm

4 5 cm, 4 cm, 6 cm

5 10 mm, 20 mm, 10 mm

6 8 m, 8 m, 8 m

7 18 mm, 50 mm, 42 mm

8 8 m, 5 m, 3 m

9 7 m, 5 m, 2 m

10 Measure to the nearest centimetre the length, width and height of a drawer. Calculate its volume.

11 Measure to the nearest centimetre the length, width and height of a shoe box. Calculate its volume.

12 An aquarium is 42 cm long, 18 cm wide, and 20 cm high. How many cubic centimetres of water will it hold?

13 The volume of a coal bunker is 3 cubic metres. The coal bunker is 3 m long and $\frac{1}{2}$ m deep. How wide is the coal bunker?

This box has a volume of
1 cubic centimetre.

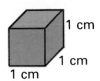

1 cm
1 cm
1 cm

It will hold **1 millilitre (mL)** of liquid.
The millilitre is used to measure
small capacities.

There are 1000 ml in a litre.

1000 ml = 1 l

This jug can be used to
measure 1 litre.

The litre is used
to measure larger
capacities.

$\frac{1}{2}$ of 1000 ml = 500 ml

$\frac{1}{4}$ l = 250 ml

$\frac{3}{4}$ l = $\frac{1}{2}$ l + $\frac{1}{4}$ l = 500 ml + 250 ml
= 750 ml

Choose the correct capacity.

1

4 millilitres
4 litres

2

1 millilitre
1 litre

3

200 millilitres
200 litres

4 (a) Collect some containers and estimate the capacity of each.
(b) Check your estimates by filling each container, then pouring the
contents into a measuring jug.

Copy and complete:

5

2l
1l

500 ml, or ___ litre

6

2l
1l

$\frac{3}{4}$ l, or ___ ml

7

2l
1l

1.5 litres, or ___ ml

8   2000 ml = ___ l

9   $1\frac{3}{4}$ l = ___ ml

10   2.4 l = ___ ml

6 l 800 ml = 6000 ml + 800 ml = 6800 ml
4 l 710 ml = 4.710 l = 4710 ml

Change to ml.

| 11 | 1 l 300 ml | 12 | 3 l 750 ml | 13 | 10 l 205 ml | 14 | 7 l |
| 15 | 1.8 l | 16 | 4.7 l | 17 | 0.9 l | 18 | 0.08 l |

2870 ml = 2000 ml + 870 ml = 2 l 870 ml

Change to l and ml. (3802 ml = 3 l 802 ml)

19   9642 ml   20   1586 ml   21   7064 ml   22   16 503 ml

23

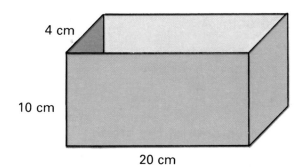

4 cm

10 cm

20 cm

A rectangular tin measures
20 cm by 10 cm by 4 cm.

(a) What is its volume in cubic centimetres?
(b) How many millimetres of water does it hold when full?
    (Remember: 1 cubic centimetre = 1 ml)
(c) What is its capacity
    in litres?

1   (a) Find the average of 4, 8, 9, 11.   (b) What is the range?

2   The average of four numbers is 10. Three of the numbers are 6, 9
    and 13. What is the other number?

Volume and capacity.

Remember that 1 cubic centimetre (cm³) equals 1 millilitre (ml) and 1000 ml = 1 litre (l).

You need a measuring glass or jug graduated in millilitres.

You also need a displacement jar.

Water is poured into the jar until it reaches level A.

If more water is then poured in, it will run out of the spout.

This water can be collected in container B.

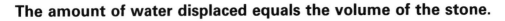

A →

Experiment

Fill the displacement jar with water up to point A.

Place a stone in the displacement jar.

Measure the amount of water that runs out into B.

(The water has been **displaced** from the jar.)

The amount of water displaced equals the volume of the stone.

For example, if 48.6 ml of water is displaced, the volume of the stone must be 48.6 cm³.

1   A key displaces 5.7 ml of water.
    What is the volume of the key?

2   A horse-shoe has a volume of 12.2 cm³.
    How many millilitres of water will it displace?

3   You need some stones of various sizes.
    Find the volume of each stone.

4   Can you think of a way of finding the volume of an object that floats?

Weight.

A cubic centimetre, or millilitre, of water weighs 1 gram (g).
The gram is used to measure small weights.
1000 g = 1 kilogram (kg)
The kilogram is used to measure heavier weights.

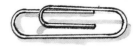

About 1 g

About 1 kg

Since there are 1000 g in 1 kg,

$100\ g = \frac{1}{10}$ of 1000 g $= \frac{1}{10}$ of 1 kg

$\quad = 0.1\ kg$

$10\ g = \frac{1}{100}$ of 1000 g $= \frac{1}{100}$ of 1 kg

$\quad = 0.01\ kg$

$\frac{1}{2}$ kg = 0.5 kg = $\frac{1}{2}$ of 1000 g = 500 g

$\frac{1}{4}$ kg = 0.25 kg = $\frac{1}{4}$ of 1000 g = 250 g

$\frac{3}{4}$ kg = $\frac{1}{2}$ kg + $\frac{1}{4}$ kg = 0.5 kg + 0.25 kg = 0.75 kg

$\quad = 500\ g + 250\ kg = 750\ g$

Copy and complete:

1  600 g = ____ kg

2  900 g = ____ kg

3 700 g = ____ kg

4 130 g = ____ kg

5 910 g = ____ kg

6 0.4 kg = ____ g

7 0.8 kg = ____ g

8 3.2 kg = ____ g

9 0.15 kg = ____ g

10 0.67 kg = ____ g

11 1.94 kg = ____ g

Choose the correct weight.

12

5 g   5 kg

13

5 g   5 kg

14

200g   200 kg

15 Weigh yourself in kilograms.

16 Estimate the weight of some objects. Check your estimates by weighing.

Graph showing cost of apples at 90p per kilogram.

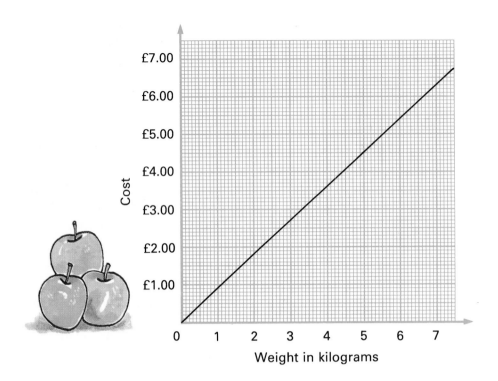

Use the graph to answer these questions.

1 How many grams does each small division on the horizontal (weight) axis represent?

2 How many pence does each small division on the vertical (cost) axis represent?

3 Use the graph to find the cost of the following weights of apples.

(a) 2 kg   (b) 3 kg   (c) 4 kg   (d) 5 kg   (e) 6 kg   (f) 7 kg

(g) 1.5 kg   (h) 2.5 kg   (i) 3.7 kg   (j) 4.9 kg   (k) 5.1 kg   (l) 6.3 kg

4 Use the graph to find the number of kilograms that can be bought for these amounts of money.

(a) £1.00   (b) £2.00   (c) £3.50   (d) £4.50   (e) £5.50   (f) £6.50

(g) £0.60   (h) £1.20   (i) £2.70   (j) £3.40   (k) £4.90   (l) £5.30

5 Check your answers to question 3 using a calculator and multiplying the number of kilograms by 90p.

6 Use a calculator to check your answers to question 4.

Thousands.

Thousands					
Hundreds	Tens	Units	Hundreds	Tens	Units
2	8	1	4	3	6

With numbers of 5 digits or more
we use a gap to
separate the thousands.

281 436

6 units or 6
3 tens or 30
4 hundreds or 400
1 thousand or 1000
8 ten thousands or 80 000
2 hundred thousands or 200 000

Here is another way to write the number:
two hundred and eighty-one thousand **four hundred and thirty-six.**

357 168

1 **Which digit is in the:**

(a) **thousands place?**   (b) **units place?**
(c) **tens place?**   (d) **ten thousands place?**
(e) **hundreds place?**   (f) **hundred thousands place?**

What does the red digit stand for?

Give two answers.

1   3**8**2 719
        ↓
        eighty thousands
        80 000

2   91 6**9**2

3   528 3**1**4

4   291 7**5**4

5   362 **8**46

6   5**5**5 555

7   **4**44 444

Write the numbers in figures.

8   Twenty-six thousand, two hundred and nineteen.

9   Four hundred and fifty-three thousand, five hundred and six.

10 Forty-five thousand, two hundred and seventy-four.

11 Two hundred and fifty-six thousand, five hundred and twenty.

12 Six hundred and thirty thousand, three hundred and six.

Give the number that is 10 000 less.

13 38 216

14 738 172

15 529 304

16 521 783

17 304 216

18 293 817

Give the number that is 1000 greater.

19 74 263

20 382 160

21 9421

22 593 741

23 529 284

24 199 263

The expanded form of 42 356 is
40 000 + 2000 + 300 + 50 + 6.

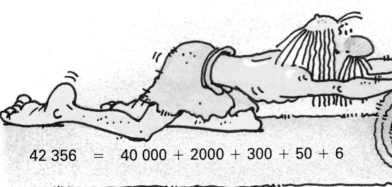

42 356   =   40 000 + 2000 + 300 + 50 + 6

Write these numbers in expanded form.

25 38 921

26 57 496

27 35 142

28 238 145

29 726 574

30 953 884

Comparing two whole numbers.

A Compare these two numbers: 7689   12 015
The number that has more digits
is the greater number.

12 015 > 7689   7689 < 12 015

B Compare these two numbers: 12 426   13 010
Both numbers have the same
number of digits.

Start at the left and
compare the digits in the
ten thousands place.
They are the same.

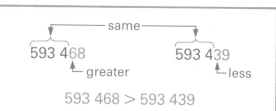

Compare the digits
in the thousands place.

13 010 > 12 426   12 426 < 13 010

749 263 749 402	593 468 593 439
749 263 < 749 402	593 468 > 593 439

Copy and complete these.
Less than (<) or greater than (>)?

1 783 ⬤ 2873   2 5934 ⬤ 5926   3 8342 ⬤ 8432

4 3999 ⬤ 4000   5 56 984 ⬤ 6884   6 34 291 ⬤ 35 384

7 72 916 ⬤ 75 388   8 26 593 ⬤ 26 504   9 391 782 ⬤ 390 700

10 458 371 ⬤ 453 871   11 100 000 ⬤ 99 999

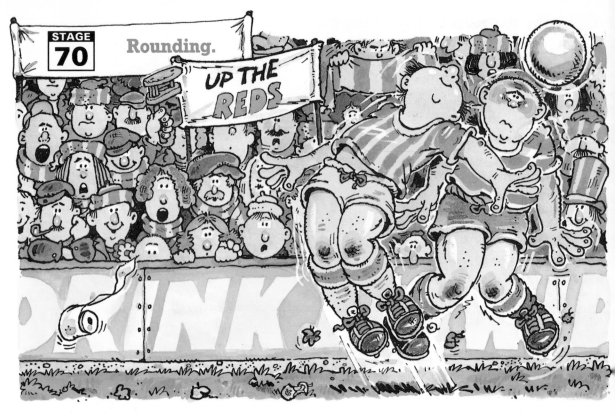

Rounding.

The greatest number of people that can be safely fitted into a football ground is called the **capacity** of the ground.

The *exact* capacity of Kingstown football ground is

50 126.

This number, rounded to the nearest thousand, is

50 000.

Here are some examples.

A   67 634 rounded to the nearest thousand is 68 000.

67 000   68 00
                  67 634

B   8435 rounded to the nearest hundred is 8400.

8400   8500
        8435

C   950 is exactly halfway between 900 and 1000.
    We round up to 1000.

900   1000
              950

Football ground	Capacity
Arsenic	62 291
Kingstown	50 126
Southamsea	59 245
Liveridge	67 510
Astonville	101 001
Tottering	59 075
Wolverton	81 455
Oxton	41 097
Bournham	60 546
Nottingbury	80 985

1 Which football ground has the greatest capacity?

2 Which has the least capacity?

3 How many football grounds can hold more than 75 000 people?

4 Round the capacity of each football ground to the nearest thousand.

5 What is the capacity of the Wolverton ground rounded to the nearest ten thousand?

6 What is the capacity of the Astonville ground rounded to the nearest ten thousand?

7 Find the difference in capacity between the grounds at Wolverton and Astonville:
(a) using the numbers in the table;
(b) using the rounded numbers found in questions 5 and 6.

Round each of these numbers to the nearest hundred.

8 743   9 695   10 850   11 4763   12 45

Round each of these numbers to the nearest ten.

13 52   14 87   15 45   16 9672   17 803

18 Round 72 869 to the nearest:
(a) ten;   (b) hundred;   (c) thousand.

a.m. is used for times after 12:00 midnight and before 12:00 noon.
p.m. is used for times after 12:00 noon and before 12:00 midnight.

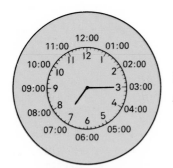

If it is morning this clock shows 7:15 a.m.
As a 24-hour clock time this is written as 07:15.

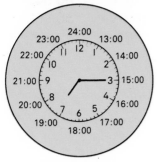

If it is evening this clock shows 7:15 p.m.
As a 24-hour clock time this is written as 19:15.

Give the time using a.m. or p.m., and also as a 24-hour clock time.

1

School dinner time.

2

School finishes.

3

Time to get up.

4

Time for bed.

5

Let's watch the
television.

6

I'm getting up early to
go fishing.

Daylight or dark?

7   **02:06**   8   **12:00 noon**   9   **15:15**   10   **12:00 midnight**

4 days 5 hours = __ hours	582 minutes = __ hours __ minutes
To change days to hours, multiply by 24.	To change minutes to hours, divide by 60.
Solution: $\begin{array}{r} 24 \\ \times\ 4 \\ \hline 96 \\ +\ 5 \\ \hline 101 \end{array}$	Solution: $\begin{array}{r} 9 \\ 60\overline{)582} \\ -540 \\ \hline 42 \end{array}$
4 days 5 hours = 101 hours	582 minutes = 9 hours 42 minutes

Multiply or divide?

11 To change minutes to seconds, __ by 60.

12 To change seconds to minutes, __ by 60.

13 To change hours to days, __ by 24.

14 To change days to hours, __ by 24.

Rewrite each record-breaking time.

15 Rocking a chair.
Time: 336 hours
        = __ days

16 Disco dancing.
Time: 36 hours 19 minutes
        = __ minutes

17 Team table-tennis playing.

Time: 22 days 4 hours
        __ weeks __ days __ hours

18 Skipping.

Time: 8 hours 35 minutes
(a) __ minutes
(b) He skipped 3540 times in the first hour. What was his average number of skips per minute in that hour?

More about time.

A group of children started a long walk at 08:40.
They planned to walk for 1 hour and 30 minutes
before taking their first break.
Here is a way to find the time when they took
their first break.

Starting
time

Add
1
hour

Break
time

Add
30
minutes

08:40

09:40

10:10

I first add 1 hour
and then add 30 minutes
to the answer.

The children started walking again at 10:25.
At 13:15 they stopped for a picnic.
Here is a way to find how long they walked
for from the end of the break to the time
they stopped for the picnic.

End of
break

1 hour

2 hours

2 hours
and 35
minutes

2 hours
and 50
minutes

10:25

11:25

12:25

13:00

13:15

Give the time that is:

1 40 minutes later than 06:15;

2 45 minutes later than 14:15;

3 19 minutes later than 09:45;

4 1 hour and 20 minutes later than 12:35;

5 2 hours and 15 minutes later than 04:08;

6 50 minutes earlier than 13:05;

7 1 hour and 40 minutes earlier than 07:30;

8 3 hours and 20 minutes earlier than 07:30.

How much time?

9 05:30 to 06:15

10 02:20 to 03:15

11 04:45 to 06:30

12 19:08 to 21:20

13 10:45 to 13:30

14 13:30 to 22:45

Solve.

15

It is 18:50.
The programme I want to watch starts in 1 hour and 10 minutes.
At what time does it start?

16

Melanie started practising at 16:40.
She practised for 1¼ hours.
What time did she finish?

17 Jan just missed the 09:07 train.
The next train is at 10:48.
How long will she have to wait?

18 John went to bed at 21:40 and got up at 07:20.
How long did he sleep?

19 On Saturday Diane and her father spent 4½ hours painting a fence.
If they started at 09:20, what time did they finish?

20 The time that Mrs Kelly works over 8 hours in a day is considered overtime. One day she worked from 07:30 to 18:25.
How much overtime did she work that day?

A timetable.

I live in Axton.

The timetable below shows
the bus times between
Axton and Bisham.

I live in London Road.

Time of departure

Axton	07:15	07:30	07:45	08:00	
Aspin Lane	07:29	07:44	07:59	08:14	
The Stag Inn	07:36	07:51	08:06	08:21	and then every
London Road	07:45	08:00	08:15	08:30	15 minutes
Rose Green	07:48	08:03	08:18	08:33	
St Ann's Church	07:51	08:06	08:21	08:36	
Bisham (arrives)	08:18	08:33	08:48	09:03	

1. How long does the bus take to travel to Bisham from:
   (a) Axton? (b) Aspin Lane? (c) London Road?
   (d) Rose Green? (e) St Ann's Church?

2. At what times between 12:05 and 15:05 do buses leave Axton?

3. At what times between 14:00 and 18:00 do buses arrive at Bisham?

4. At what time is the 10:15 from Axton due at:
   (a) Aspin Lane? (b) The Stag Inn? (c) London Road?
   (d) Rose Green? (e) St Ann's Church? (f) Bisham?

5. Diana has to be at The Stag Inn by 09:25.
   What is the latest time she can leave Axton?

6. Stephen has to be in Bisham before 10:00.
   What is the latest time he can leave London Road?

7. The Reverend Cross lives in Aspin Lane.
   He has to christen a baby at 11:00 in St Ann's Church, but he needs to be
   at the church 20 minutes before the christening.
   What is the latest time he can leave Aspin Lane?

8 Diana caught the 09:00 bus from Axton but it was 9 minutes late.
At what time would it arrive at the other stops if it did not lose any more
time and did not regain any of the lost time?

9 Stephen catches the 08:00 from London Road to Bisham every day to go
to school. The return journey takes the same time as the journey to school.
(a) What amount of time does he spend on the bus each day?
(b) What amount of time does he spend travelling in a school week?
(c) There are 40 weeks in the school year.
    How many hours does he spend travelling during that time if he does
    not miss a day of school?

10 The distance from Axton to London Road is 21 km.
(a) What is the average speed of the bus between these two places?
(b) At this speed, how far would the bus travel in 20 minutes?

11 Work with a friend. You need your local bus timetable.
Make up some questions like those on page 70 and this page.
Give them to your friend to answer.
You answer your friend's questions.

keeping skills sharp

1 2.4 cm = __ mm	2 4.6 km = __ m	3 80 cm = __ m
4 7.9 kg = __ g	5 400 g = __ kg	6 1.9 l = __ ml

Measurement puzzles.

1 **Area**

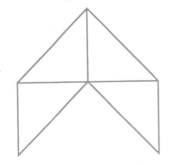

There are four right-angled triangles.
The sides containing right angles are
2 cm long.

(a) Trace the figure and cut out the four
triangles.

Rearrange them to make a rectangle.
What is the area of the rectangle?

(b) Rearrange the four triangles to make

(i) a triangle (ii) a square (iii) a parallellogram
like this

(c) What is the area of each shape?

(d) What do you notice about these areas? Can you explain this?

2 **Length**

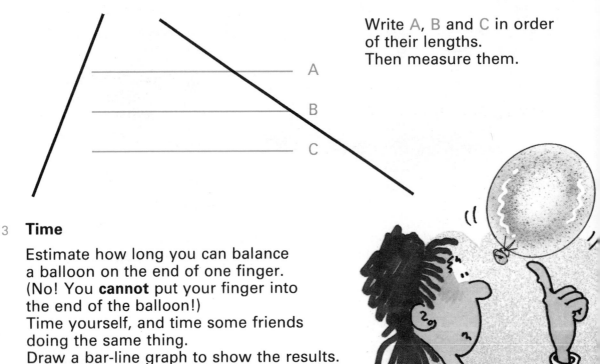

Write A, B and C in order
of their lengths.
Then measure them.

A

B

C

3 **Time**

Estimate how long you can balance
a balloon on the end of one finger.
(No! You **cannot** put your finger into
the end of the balloon!)
Time yourself, and time some friends
doing the same thing.
Draw a bar-line graph to show the results.

4 **Measurement alphabet**

Start with A and write down a measurement word that begins with A,
then a measurement word beginning with B and so on for as many of the
letters of the alphabet as you can.

1   Complete

$$\frac{1}{5} - \frac{1}{10} = \underline{}$$

2   Copy.
Write $>$ or $<$ in the ◯ .

$$\frac{3}{4} \quad ◯ \quad \frac{7}{8}$$

3   (a) $153 - (10 \times 7) =$

(b) $200 \div (16 - 11) =$

4   Calculate the shaded angle between the hands of the clock.

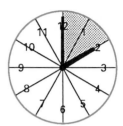

5   Measure this angle.

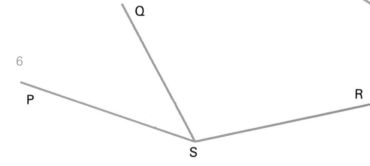

6

Angle PSR = 150 °
Angle PSQ = 43 °

Calculate angle QSR.

Write: Angle QSR =

7   An aircraft is flying on a bearing of 193°. It turns through an angle of 89° in a clockwise direction. What is its bearing now?

8   (a)   What is the average of 19, 26 and 36?

(b)   What is the range?

9   Find the cost of 3 pens at 29p each and 7 pencils at 18p each.

10   Annie had £20. She bought 3 newspapers costing 27p each and a magazine costing 96p.

(a)   How much did she spend?

(b)   How much did she have left?

11   Calculate the area of a rectangle with length 37 cm and width 8 cm.

12   Draw the net of a closed cube.

13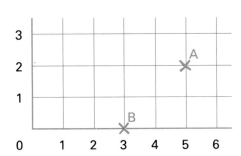

(a) What is the number pair for A?

(b) What is the number pair for B?

14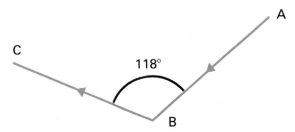

Imagine you are walking along AB and reach B. What angle must you turn through to face in the direction of C?

15 Write this number.
6 in the hundredths place
2 in the units place
9 in the tens place
3 in the tenths place

16 Complete these patterns.

(a)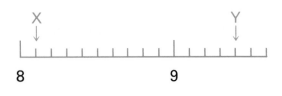

(b) 0, 1, 3, 6, 10, __, __

17   4.59
  + 6.77
  _____

18   41.2
  − 18.5
  _____

19   9.64
  − 2.89
  _____

20 67.9 + 38

21 4.6 + 5.83

22 30.4 − 19

23 11.2 − 5.81

24 Round 8.94 to:

(a) one place of decimals;

(b) the nearest whole number.

25 Give the values at X and Y as decimals.

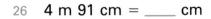

26 4 m 91 cm = ____ cm

27 Calculate the volume of this cuboid.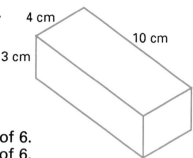

4 cm

10 cm

3 cm

28 6 and 12 are the first two multiples of 6.
Write down the next four multiples of 6.

29 Write any multiple of 8 that is also a multiple of 3.

30 $\begin{array}{r} 296 \\ \times\ \ 10 \\ \hline \end{array}$ 31 $\begin{array}{r} 391 \\ \times\ 100 \\ \hline \end{array}$ 32 Use a calculator to find the
number of pages in 29 books
if each book has 64 pages.

33 How many days are there from June 26th to July 17th? (Don't count both
days.)

34 Give each quotient and remainder.

(a) $9\overline{)87}$ (b) $5\overline{)73}$

35 Find the average of 56, 69 and 85.

36 Find the total cost of 5 kg of apples at 46p a kilogram and 7 kg of pears at
57p a kilogram.

37 You can use the numbers 1, 7 and 6 **in that order**, and any mathematics
signs you like, to make numbers. For example $17 - 6 = 11$, $1 + (7 \times 6) = 43$.
Make four other numbers.

38 Measure these lengths in millimetres.

(a)

(b)

39 Measure this angle.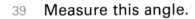

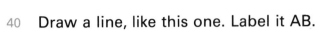

40 Draw a line, like this one. Label it AB.

   (a) Draw a line parallel to AB.

   (b) Draw a line perpendicular to AB.

41 The dashed lines are lines of symmetry.
Copy this, and draw the missing parts of the shape.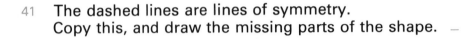

42 What is the order of rotational symmetry of this shape?

43 Draw a rectangle with sides of 4.9 cm and 1.3 cm.

44 Draw a triangle with sides of 46 mm, 49 mm and 34 mm.

45 Complete this net of a pyramid with a rectangular base.

46 Choose one of these for each of your answers:
A No chance, B Poor chance, C Even chance, D Good chance, E Certain

   (a) I will be a doctor.

   (b) I will die if I stop eating and drinking.

47 A line in a bar-line graph is 3 cm long. It represents 15 children.

   (a) How long would the line be, to represent 25 children?

   (b) If the line was 4 cm long, how many children would it represent?

48 Write the temperatures at A and B.

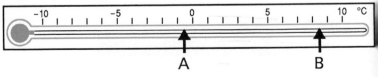

49 The tallies show the number of goals scored in two seasons.

Season A ~~IIII~~ ~~IIII~~ ~~IIII~~ ~~IIII~~ II

Season B ~~IIII~~ ~~IIII~~ ~~IIII~~ ~~IIII~~ ~~IIII~~ III

(a) Find the total numbers of goals scored in the two seasons.

(b) Find the average number of goals scored in a season.

50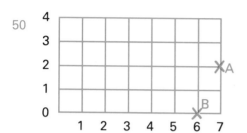

(a) What are the coordinates of A?

(b) What are the coordinates of B?

51 Plan a 'tuck shop' for your class. Think about what you would have in your shop, and what you would charge for these things.

52 At three different points on a road a motorist came to a 'fork', and had to decide whether to go left (L) or right (R). Copy and complete the tree diagrams to show the choices.

First fork   L   R
                           /   \   /   \
Second fork   LL   LR   RL   ____
                  / \   / \   / \   / \
Third fork   LLL   LLR   ____   ____   ____   ____   ____   ____

53 Use a calculator to do this calculation. Round your answer to the nearest whole number.

$(16 \div 3) \times 21$

54 What part of the large square is shaded?

Give your answer as:

(a) a fraction in lowest terms;

(b) a percentage.

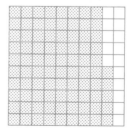

55 Write $\frac{17}{20}$ as a percentage.

56 A book costs £20 but a 5% reduction was given in a sale.
    What was the sale price?

57 A car's tank holds 70 litres of petrol when full. It has 12.7 litres in it.
    How much more petrol is needed to fill the tank?

58 A number is multiplied by 3 and then 2 is added.
    The result is 26. What was the number?

59   19 m 46 cm   60   9.20 km
      + 43 m 84 cm   − 6.75 km
    _____   _____

61 Find the perimeter of   62 Find the volume of this cuboid.
    this rectangle.

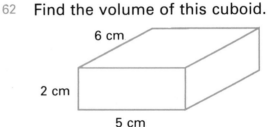

63 Change 4 l 28 ml to millilitres.

64 Change 4.370 kg to grams.

65 What number is 10 000 more than 419 387?

66 500 000 + 6000 + 200 + 9 =

67 Round 44 482 to: (a) the nearest 100;   (b) the nearest 1000.

68 Write 6:36 p.m. as 24-hour clock time.

69 Change 4 hours 53 minutes to minutes.

70 How many minutes are there
    between the times shown?